G000057343

Jonathan Wood

SHIRE PUBLICATIONS

Published in Great Britain in 2014 by Shire Publications Ltd,
PO Box 883, Oxford OX1 9PL, United Kingdom.
PO Box 3985, New York, NY 10185-3983, USA.
E-mail: shire@shirebooks.co.uk   www.shirebooks.co.uk

A CIP catalog record for this book is available from the
British Library

Shire Library no. 465   •   ISBN-13: 978 0 74780 674 5

Jonathan Wood has asserted his right under the Copyright,
Designs and Patents Act, 1988, to be identified as the
author of this book.

Designed by Ken Vail Graphic Design, Cambridge, UK,
and typeset in Perpetua and Gill Sans.
Printed in China through World Print Ltd.

14 15 16 17 18   12 11 10 9 8 7 6 5

COVER IMAGE
A reproduction of a Harold Connolly illustration of an MG
M-type Midget from a 1930 edition of *Motor* magazine.

TITLE PAGE IMAGE
A mechanic points out the advantages of buying an MG *TF*
to a prospective customer. Introduced for the 1954 season,
this was the final member of the T-series family with its
essentially pre-war styling enhanced by integral headlamps
and lower lines.

CONTENTS PAGE IMAGE
This 18/80 graced MG's stand at the 1928 Motor Show
and was the second of three experimental cars. It is being
driven in a Bugatti Owners' Club 1931 speed trial at
Chalfont St Peter, Buckinghamshire, by John Thornley,
who joined MG in 1931 and ran the company in the post-
war years. This car was subsequently bought by his father.

ACKNOWLEDGEMENTS
One of the pleasures of writing about MG over the past
thirty or so years is that it has brought me into contact
with plenty of MG people, although, inevitably, many of
them have since died. Thanks are therefore due to John
Thornley, Syd Enever, Roy Brocklehurst, Don Hayter,
Ted Lund, Jack Daniels, Ted Lee and, more recently,
Gerry McGovern, Brian Griffin and Nick Fell.

I would like to thank the following for supplying
illustrations: Barry Blight, Neill Bruce, David Hutchison
of the Early MG Society, the late John Seager, Robin
Barraclough, Gary Perry of the MG Car Club's SVW
Register, the MGCC's MGA Register Archives, Piers
Hubbard, Peter Seymour, Brian Wright, the MG Owners'
Club, Peter Card and Simon Wittenberg of Automotive
PR. The remainder of the photographs are from the
author's collection. Assistance was also kindly provided
by Malcolm Green, Peter Neal and Brian Folkard.

Shire Publications is supporting the Woodland Trust, the UK's leading woodland conservation charity, by funding the dedication of trees.

CONTENTS

STYLE THEN SPEED

THE location was the city of Nanjing, China, and the date 27th March 2007 when the latest act in the turbulent history of the MG sports car was played out. There Nanjing Automobile proudly unveiled its Chinese-built MG TF that was initially intended for sale in the Far East.

Although the days of the British indigenous motor industry as a volume producer have now passed, MG has survived no fewer than eight changes of corporate ownership since its emergence in the mid-1920s.[1]

MG stands for Morris Garages, and it was in 1922 that the thirty-four-year-old Cecil Kimber was appointed general manager of this Oxford-based business. Manchester-born Kimber had studied accountancy and worked for a number of car companies before joining Morris. But he also possessed a strong artistic flair, probably inherited from his mother, who was a keen amateur painter, and this talent was to express itself through his ability to design car bodywork of quality and distinction.

The roots of the Morris Garages reach back to 1910, although the Cowley-domiciled William Morris had begun selling cars in the city back in 1902. Drawing on this experience, in 1913 he launched the Morris Oxford, the model with the distinctive Bullnose-shaped radiator, which evolved into the four-seater Cowley of 1915. It was to become the bestselling British car of the 1920s.

Although it might have been a trifle pedestrian on account of its no-frills 1.5 litre side-valve engine, the Bullnose was also available in more expensive Oxford form and Kimber used both versions as the basis of his first special-bodied Morris. The Morris Garages Chummy was introduced for the 1923 season and a total of 109 were produced. It was a good start.

Opposite:
The Speed Model 18/80 was very much in the spirit of the Bentley and capable of speeds approaching 80 mph (129 km/h). It was drawn by Frederick Gordon Crosby for The Autocar and dates from late 1930.

---

[1] William Morris, later Lord Nuffield, 1924–35; Morris Motors, 1935–52; British Motor Corporation, 1952–68; British Leyland Motor Corporation, 1968–75; Nationalised (Leyland Cars, BL Cars, The Rover Group), 1975–88; British Aerospace, 1988–94; BMW, 1994–2000; MG Rover, 2000–4; Nanjing Automobile Corporation, 2004 to date.

Top: Kimber's first attempt at a special-bodied Morris was the Chummy of October 1922. An occasional four, it was offered on the 11.9 hp Cowley and Oxford chassis, with the latter also available in 13.9 hp form. In this now rare brochure Kimber wrote: 'To the enthusiast the Chummy body makes an ideal sports car. Its lines are graceful and sporting.' It was mounted on a 'Morris sports chassis' and finished in pastel blue.

The Charm of the Chummy Body !

255 Guineas.

Complete on a Morris-Cowley four-seater chassis with self-starter and full equipment.

Middle: MG's creator, Cecil Kimber, pictured in his first-floor office at Abingdon in the early 1930s. From this vantage point he was able to overlook much of the MG factory.

Bottom: The first MG? Oliver Arkell bought this Raworth-bodied yellow and black Morris Cowley, initiated by Cecil Kimber, in August 1923. It was described as an 'MG Super Sports Morris'.

A friend of Kimber's, Russel Chiesman, putting up a spirited performance in his 14/28 MG in the 1926 London to Land's End Trial, in which he won a silver medal.

The success of the Chummy encouraged Kimber to be more ambitious. He commissioned Raworth, an Oxford coachbuilder, to produce six open two-seater bodies for the Cowley chassis. These were painted in bright colours and the first, a yellow car with black wings, found its first customer on 11th August 1923. Oliver Arkell has the distinction of having bought the first 'MG' although the cars were not so named until 1924.

The high Flatnose radiator of the contemporary Morris did not lend itself to Kimber's special coachwork in the same way as its Bullnose predecessor. The MG Super Sports 14/28 was on sale during the 1927 season. It was followed by the 14/40 for 1928.

This was accorded to the Morris Oxford 14/28-based MG Super Sports. Offered with a choice of coachwork for the 1925 season, it was best-known as a four-seater tourer of polished aluminium by Carbodies of Coventry. The price was £395, a significant £135 more than the Morris equivalent. Although these 1.8 litre cars were, in essence, mechanically standard, a total of 336 of all types were produced at various Oxford locations.

When Morris Motors replaced the Bullnose with the even more popular but less memorable 'Flatnose' version for 1927, Kimber had little choice but

MG's famous octagonal badge was designed in 1923 by Cecil Kimber's cost accountant, Ted Lee. The chocolate and cream combination was, the writer believes, inspired by the livery of the Great Western Railway, which served Oxford at the time.

This fine study of an 18/80 in May 1929 is by The Autocar's resident artist Frederick Gordon Crosby, himself an 18/80 owner.

to follow suit, even though the new radiator lacked the character of the original.

Kimber's ongoing success was formalised by William Morris in March 1928. Then he registered The MG Car Company (Proprietors The Morris Garages) as a separate entity and, for the time being, it remained his personal property.

Until that year every MG had clearly reflected its Morris origins. But, in August 1928, came the 18/80 which can be regarded as the first true MG, since it had its own distinctive radiator, also the work of the talented Kimber. Priced at £485 in touring form, it was effectively a scaled-down Bentley sports car, powered by a potent 2.5 litre six-cylinder Morris overhead camshaft engine. Capable of a spirited 75 mph (120 km/h), the 18/80 was to remain in production until 1933.

The handsome 'six' was not the only new model to grace MG's stand at the 1928 Motor Show. In the same August of the six's appearance, Morris had launched his answer to the baby Austin Seven in the form of the 847cc Minor saloon. Under its bonnet was a diminutive, lively but sophisticated four-cylinder overhead camshaft engine, built by Wolseley, which had joined the Morris stable in 1927.

Kimber immediately recognised its sports-car potential; he intuitively preferred small cars, being relatively slight in build and 5 feet 5 inches (165 cm) tall.

This 18/80 graced MG's stand at the 1928 Motor Show and was the second of three experimental cars. It is being driven in a Bugatti Owners' Club 1931 speed trial at Chalfont St Peter, Buckinghamshire, by John Thornley, who joined MG in 1931 and ran the company in the post-war years. This car was subsequently bought by his father.

The outcome was the Minor-based M-type Midget, enhanced by a light, distinctive two-seater fabric body with a pointed tail in the manner of Grand Prix racers of the day.

Priced at a competitive £175, the Midget represented the beginnings of an MG model line that was to survive until 1955. Happiest at about 50 mph (80 km/h), though capable of more, the model was an immediate success. Production began in March 1929 and continued until June 1932, by which time 3,235 examples had been completed. This made it far and away the world's most popular sports car.

It was largely through the success of the Midget that MG was in need of a new home, having operated from a purpose-built factory at Cowley since 1927. Kimber found an empty works at Abingdon, some 7 miles (11 km) from Oxford. MG moved there in September 1929 and the Thames-side town was destined to remain its home until 1980.

At about the time of the move, the Wall Street financial crash occurred in America, heralding the onset of the world Depression. Sales of the expensive 18/80 were badly affected, although demand for the small, economical M-type continued apace.

MG's racing credentials were becoming fast established. It had won the team prize in the 1930 Double-Twelve race at Brooklands, the prestigious British equivalent of the Le Mans twenty-four-hour event.

The M-type of 1928 was MG's first big seller. The distinctive and light fabric two-seater body was built by Carbodies, which charged MG just £6 10s (£6.50) apiece! Published in December 1930, this painting is the work of Harold Connolly, who also assisted Kimber in the design of MG coachwork.

"The Competition Favourite"——

The MG

Then, in February 1931, Captain George Eyston, driving a special M-type coded EX 120, achieved a speed of 103.13 mph (165.96 km/h) at the Montlhéry circuit near Paris. Its chassis was new, the rear members of which ran beneath, rather than above, the rear axle. MG's fame was soon to spread far beyond its native Britain, as Kimber embarked on an extensive programme of racing and record-breaking.

Such competition achievements had not been attained by accident. A good picker of subordinates, Kimber had recruited Hubert Charles, a Morris production specialist who had been unofficially contributing to MG's mechanical specifications since 1925. He now became chief engineer. Unusually for the Morris company, Charles was a graduate, having obtained a BSc degree in engineering from London University.

Given a free hand by Kimber, Charles's talent soon found expression in the C-type Midget, announced in April 1931, its mechanicals inspired by EX 120. With engine capacity reduced to 746cc, to bring it into the 750cc racing class, it sold for £295, or £345 if equipped with a Powerplus supercharger.

With external exhaust and double-humped speed-deflecting cockpit cowls in the manner of the record-breaker, the C-type was the ideal budget road-racer. And its competition credentials were assured when examples were placed first and third in the 1931 Tourist Trophy race, a handicap event.

In August 1932 MG introduced one of its greatest sports cars, the J2 Midget, which replaced the popular M-type. Kimber excelled himself with its lines and, it should be said, he was aided in this work by Harold Connolly, a talented artist who since 1929 had illustrated MG's catalogues.

The M-type was also available in Sportsman's Coupé form and was clearly aimed at the ladies. A total of 493 were built between 1929 and 1932.

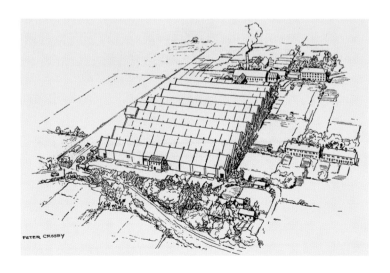

Abingdon, Berkshire (from 1974 in Oxfordshire), was MG's home from 1929 until the factory's closure in 1980. The works were subsequently extended on the fields to the left during the Second World War. Cecil Kimber's office is in the right background.

Right: The J2
chassis of 1932.
Notable features
are the remote
control gear lever
that fell readily to
hand and the
underslung chassis.

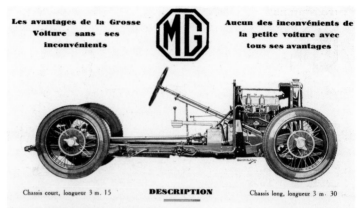

Right: The J2 chassis of 1932. Notable features are the remote control gear lever that fell readily to hand and the underslung chassis.

Like the C-type, it possessed the now-distinctive humped scuttle, together with cutaway doors and an exposed slab petrol tank with a spare wheel purposefully exposed to view at the rear. Although the wings were originally of the cycle type, from 1933 the fronts and rears were gracefully united by rudimentary running boards. They completed the definitive MG look that was to endure until 1955.

Mechanically the J2 perpetuated the 847cc capacity of its predecessor while the chassis followed the C-type's specification. This ensured a top speed of around 65 mph (105 km/h), although *The Autocar* recorded 80.35 mph (129.30 km/h) in a specially prepared car!

The styling of the L-type Magna Continental Coupé for 1934 was inspired by Bugatti's fiacre coachwork, which in its turn reflected the influence of horse-drawn carriages. Powered by a 1,100cc six-cylinder engine, the Coupé was destined to be a slow-selling variant.

The shape of the definitive MG sports car arrived in 1932 with the J2. Note that it was marketed as 'A Man's Car!'

The New **MG** *Midget*
"A Man's Car!"

Below: The K3 Magnette of 1933 was MG's most successful racing car and was the first to be fitted with a pre-selector gearbox as standard. This is Jock Manby-Colegrave's car (K3004), pictured prior to that year's Tourist Trophy race, where he was placed seventh. Mechanic Percy Kemish is at the wheel.

The Type N Magnette open four-seater of 1934 was powered by a 1.3 litre six-cylinder engine, courtesy of the Magnette KD of the previous year. The chassis was new with an 8 foot (2438 mm) wheelbase.

The new M.G. MAGNETTE Type 'N'

and The M.G. MAGNETTE K.N. Type Saloon

Last of the 847cc overhead camshaft Midgets, the much improved P-type of 1934 differed from its predecessors in using a three-bearing crankshaft engine, bequeathed in essence to the Q and R-type racers. Its PB successor of 1935/6 was powered by a bigger-bored 939cc unit.

A total of 2,083 examples of the J2 were completed by the time it was replaced in January 1934 by the slightly roomier P-type. This was outwardly similar but its wheelbase was increased by $1\,^3/_{16}$ inches. Mechanically, a limiting factor of the engine had been its two-bearing crankshaft, which was prone to breakages. This deficiency was redressed by the introduction of a centre main bearing, which made for smoother running and permitted greater tuning potential.

In June 1935 it made way for the PB, whereupon its predecessor became the PA. The new version differed in having a radiator enhanced with coloured slats which echoed the upholstery. This feature had first appeared on the Mark II version of the 18/80 in 1931.

Under the bonnet, the PB engine was subject to changes, capacity having been increased to 939cc. This assured better performance to 70 mph

Coventry coachbuilder Charlesworth was responsible for the touring version of the SA. This 1938 season model saw the spare wheel transferred from the rear of the car to the front wing and cutaways being made to the front doors.

(112 km/h). The model was destined for a life of only eight months, being discontinued in February 1936. Total production of both P-types amounted to some 2,500 cars.

Had Kimber been content to build just four-cylinder models, MG would undoubtedly have remained profitable. But he also launched what was destined to be a bewildering range of small six-cylinder cars and, apart from the 1.3 litre F-type Magna of 1932, the first of the family, which sold 1,250 examples, the Magnette and related lines were built only in their hundreds. They did, however, spawn MG's most successful racing car of the decade: the K3 Magnette of 1933.

Thirty-three examples of this supercharged 1,087cc two-seater were produced and the K3 cemented MG's reputation as a serious contender in international competition.

A trio was entered in the 1933 Mille Miglia race, two being placed first and second in their class in this famous Italian event. MG also won the team prize. And in the same year Tazio Nuvolari, the greatest driver of the day, triumphed in the Tourist Trophy race. In fact MGs would have taken the first four places, had it not been for a lone Alfa Romeo having come third. A K3 also won the demanding 500 Miles race of 1933 at Brooklands at an average speed of 106.53 mph (171.43 km/h).

The model then swept the board, taking the first five places at the 1934 Mannin Beg event in the Isle of Man, but this triumph was overshadowed by tragedy for MG. Frankie Tayler, a twenty-seven-year-old racing mechanic who had joined Morris Garages in 1923, was killed during an unofficial practice for the event. The driver, Kaye Don, who had also entered his K3,

The SA was replaced for 1939 by the outwardly similar WA and its 2.6 litre engine developed 95.5 bhp, not quite the 105 bhp shown here!

The WA possessed a well-appointed interior, although some artistic licence is apparent. Note the comfortable rear seat, complete with arm rest, and corner head rest.

was charged with manslaughter and served a four-month prison sentence. The event distressed MG's owner, Lord Nuffield (Morris having been so elevated in 1934), and thereafter he became increasingly disenchanted with motor racing.

The 1.5 litre VA was introduced in 1937 and was good for 80 mph (129 km/h) although most were probably driven more slowly!

FOLLY BRIDGE, OXFORD.

The car that had come second in Nuvolari's celebrated 1933 TT victory was not a K3 but the supercharged four-cylinder J4 racer, which had replaced the C-type in 1932. There was also a potent road-going version, the J3, with 72 bhp under its bonnet.

It was replaced by the Q-type of 1934, which was capable of 120 mph (192 km/h), being powered by a 113 bhp engine, its output boosted by the fitment of a Zoller supercharger. It had the distinction of being the most powerful example of any pre-war car engine, developing the equivalent of 151 bhp per litre.

The Q's engine was, in truth, too fast for its traditional chassis, a deficiency addressed in the next competition MG, which was destined to be a technical tour de force. Hubert Charles's R-type of April 1935 followed Grand Prix cars of the day in being a single-seater, which meant that there could be no immediate road-going equivalent. It inherited the Q's 747cc engine but the chassis bristled with ingenuity, being a light backbone with all independent suspension, by torsion bars. This was something that no comparable MG, or any other British road car for that matter, offered.

The R-type experienced teething problems in that it rolled excessively on corners, but they remained unresolved because in July 1935 MG withdrew from racing. Lord Nuffield had, as already noted, become disillusioned with such activities and the decision was an inevitable consequence of MG being acquired in that month by Morris Motors. The Abingdon drawing office was a victim of this corporate realignment.

What happened when an MG VA Tickford drophead coupé collided with a London lamp post in the 1950s. Note the optional built-in Jackall hydraulic jack. Only 564 examples of this variant were built. Whatever happened to this one?

The decision was driven by Nuffield's financial advisers, who were fearful, in the event of his demise, of excessive death duties due on the businesses that he personally owned, of which MG was one. The policy was implemented by Leonard Lord, his young, combative managing director. But Nuffield was to clash with him in 1936. Lord left and later, in 1938, he joined the rival Austin company.

MG was, in any event, heading for a record loss of £28,156 in 1935. In the five years between 1930 and 1934 the total surplus amounted to only £419.

The car range, which now became more closely related mechanically to Morris and Wolseley models, was greatly simplified. Although Kimber's stylistic hand was readily apparent, design would thereafter emanate from Morris Motors' headquarters at Cowley. Hubert Charles remained but he ceased to have direct responsibility for MG models.

The potent but expensive overhead camshaft engines were replaced by cheaper Morris pushrod units. In October 1935 MG unveiled a very different type of car in the form of the SA, although Abingdon had been contemplating such a model prior to the change of its corporate status.

The TB Midget was produced between April and October 1939 and was the first MG to be powered by Morris Engines' 1.2 litre XPAG ohv unit. The TB was to form the basis of the post-war TC.

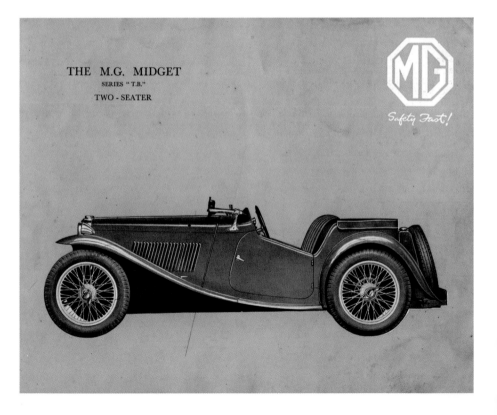

THE M.G. MIDGET
SERIES " T.B."
TWO - SEATER

Safety Fast!

This was a roomy and rapid sports saloon, no less, created to check the growing influence of the the small SS company (later Jaguar). Powered by a 2.3 litre six-cylinder engine, it was good for over 80 mph (129 km/h). There was also a handsome drophead coupé version by Tickford.

After 2,738 had been completed, it was replaced for 1939 by a derivative, the 2.7 litre WA, a comfortable and well-appointed fleet-footed express that could be wound up to speeds in excess of 90 mph (149 km/h).

There was also the VA of 1937, a 1.5 litre model on a similar theme which also survived until 1939 and also had SS (later Jaguar) firmly in its sights.

The sports cars were not neglected, however, and in March 1936 the TA Midget appeared, which inherited the lines of its PB predecessor but was rather larger. It was powered by a 1.3 litre Wolseley-related pushrod engine and was good for 75 mph (120 km/h). The public liked it and a total of 3,003 were sold by 1939. Replaced that year by the outwardly similar TB, it used a 1.2 litre engine of Morris 10 parentage.

MG production ceased with the outbreak of the Second World War in 1939 and would not re-start until its ending in 1945. Some 21,428 cars had been completed since 1924 and the post-1935 strategy had seen production levels substantially increased. What would the years of peace bring to MG and its Abingdon factory?

Goldie Gardner takes EX 135, which began life as the Magic Magnette of 1934 (see page 12), to over 200 mph (321 km/h) on the Dessau autobahn in Germany in June 1939. Its new body was the work of Reid Railton, who had John Cobb's Railton land-speed record car to his credit.

PUBLICATION No. H. & E. 5310

speed

new

T·F·SERIES MG

WHEELS FOR THE WORLD

THE world that greeted MG in 1945 was very different from the last year of peace in 1939. Most significantly, MG's founder and chief stylist, Cecil Kimber, was no longer there, having been dismissed by Lord Nuffield in November 1941, ostensibly for adopting an individual rather than collective approach to war work.

Kimber's domestic life, however, had been in some turmoil: his first wife had died in 1938 and he soon afterwards secretly married a woman with whom he had been romantically attached since 1933. This reached the ears of a disapproving Lady Nuffield...

Sadly, over three years after his dismissal, Kimber was one of two people to die in a freak railway accident outside King's Cross Station in London on 4th February 1945 at the age of only fifty-six.

Kimber's influence lived on in the memorable styling of the TC Midget, introduced in September 1945, the pre-war TB having been mildly updated. Production began in September 1945, although this was an unashamedly pre-war car with its lines firmly rooted in the 1930s.

The five years of war meant there was a pent-up worldwide demand for cars. Britain was effectively bankrupted by the war so the Labour government of the day directed the country's industries, including the motor manufacturers, to export their products to generate much-needed revenue.

Exports had previously played a relatively minor role in MG's pre-war affairs but, initially, overseas sales were confined to the pre-war Empire markets. Then American ex-servicemen began to take MGs home with them and open two-seater motoring began to catch on there, the US having no sports cars of its own. The TC, able comfortably to attain 70 mph (112 km/h), soon became popular among the Hollywood set; producer Billy Wilder was an owner, while stars Robert Stack, Yvonne De Carlo and Bette Davis were pictured with their MGs.

Demand from the United States, in particular, resulted in MG's output soaring in the post-war years, with transatlantic sales soon accounting for some 80 per cent of production.

Opposite:
Although today the TF of 1954/5 is the most sought-after of the T-series cars, it was, in truth, a dated concept at the time of its announcement in October 1953.

Although this photograph was taken in 1946, stylistically and mechanically the TC, introduced in 1945, was rooted in the 1930s. The majority, totalling 65 per cent, were exported, with America emerging in 1947 as the principal export market. A total of 1,820 TCs were sold there.

In 1947 the TC was joined by the Y-type saloon. Effectively a replacement for the pre-war VA, it was related to the Morris 10, was well appointed and capable of a rather breathless 70 mph (112 km/h). It also had the virtue of being the first MG road car to feature independent front suspension.

Also pre-war in spirit, the well-equipped Y-type saloon of 1947 was built until 1953. Its chassis, underslung at the rear, and enhanced with independent front suspension, formed the basis of the TD Midget of 1950.

The TD arrived for 1950 and, with some 30,000 built, was destined to be the best selling of the T-series cars. MG's Safety Fast slogan dated from 1929 and was coined by publicity manager George Tuck.

The Y-type's chassis, although shortened, formed the basis of the TC's successor, the TD, which was introduced in November 1949. As such it came complete with its disc wheels rather than the more traditional pre-war knock-off wires, their absence being mourned by some enthusiasts.

If the TC had introduced America to MG, then the TD consolidated this foothold and demand for this charming but dated car leapt. Whereas some 10,000 TCs were built, three times that number of TDs had left Abingdon by the time production ceased in August 1953.

In the meantime MG was overtaken by corporate events. In 1952 what had become the Nuffield Organisation was effectively absorbed by the rival Austin Company to form the British Motor Corporation (BMC). At its head was Leonard Lord, who had so radically altered MG's corporate status back in 1935.

George Eyston with record-breaker EX 179. In August 1954, powered by an unannounced 1,496cc version of the XPAG engine, iit broke eight Class F records up to 153.69 mph (247.33 km/h) at the Bonneville Salt Flats, Utah, USA. The 'record-breaking' power unit was then fitted in the TF.

The Italian-inspired Z Magnette of 1953 was closely related to the Wolseley 4/44 of the previous year, but it was more than an exercise in badge engineering. Designed by Gerald Palmer, who was also responsible for the technically and stylistically advanced Jowett Javelin, the Magnette was conceived from the start as an MG. This ZB was one of the very last of these attractive saloon cars to be assembled at Abingdon.

Below: John Thornley (*left*), MG's general manager from 1952 until 1969. Next to him in this 1963 photograph is Syd Enever, chief engineer from 1954 until 1971. On the right is his predecessor, Hubert Charles, who held the post between 1929 and 1935.

By this time the company was desperately in need of a new sports car, but Lord initiated a new make – the Austin Healey – which became an in-house rival, even though MG had a modern model, coded EX 175, waiting in the wings. It was therefore forced to soldier on with the ageing T-series line.

The TF Midget was launched in September 1953, resembling its predecessor but with its styling mildly reworked with a sloping radiator, lower bonnet line and headlights integral with the front wings. Although initially the TD's 1,250cc engine was carried over, from late 1954 it was enlarged to 1,466cc.

MG resorted to record-breaking to keep the name in the public eye, thanks to the indefatigable Lieutenant Colonel Goldie Gardner, who broke his first MG record in 1931 and his last in 1952 at the age of sixty-two. George Eyston, another MG stalwart, was similarly active.

The first tangible evidence of BMC's involvement in MG's affairs became apparent when the ZA Magnette saloon, a replacement for the Y-type, was announced in September 1953. Although the company had relied on Morris engines since its inception, this model was the first of the line to be powered by an Austin unit, this BMC B-series engine having a capacity of 1,489cc. The Magnette was to survive until 1958, and in 1956 was uprated in ZB form.

By this time MG had a new general manager, John Thornley having been promoted to the position in 1952. Formerly a trainee chartered accountant, articulate and diplomatic, Thornley, appointed in 1931 by Cecil Kimber, had in pre-war days been MG's service manager.

Thornley's powers of persuasion were much in evidence when he succeeded in convincing Leonard Lord that MG should once again be in charge of its own destiny. As a result the Abingdon drawing office, closed by Lord nineteen years before, was re-opened in 1954. By this time the company had a new chief engineer in the shape of Syd Enever, who had joined the Morris Garages as a fourteen-year-old errand boy in 1920. He proved to be an outstanding and wholly intuitive engineer.

Enever and his small team were soon at work, the production version of the design being coded EX 182. Audaciously, Thornley planned to launch it at the 1955 Le Mans twenty-four-hour race to be held in June. In the event, a strike at Pressed Steel, which produced the bodies, meant that the launch was delayed until September 1955.

So three hand-built prototypes, unnamed but bearing the factory pre-production EX number, were entered for the race. Two of the MGs finished, in twelfth and seventeenth positions, although one crashed.

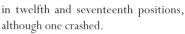

The car was named the MGA, the company having 'run out of alphabet' with the arrival of the Z-type Magnette. It was as modern in appearance as the T-series had been archaic. Inspired by the Jaguar XK120 roadster, the MGA was also styled by the versatile Syd Enever,

The line-up of three MGs, entered under their Abingdon EX 182 project number, at Le Mans in 1955. Number 41 in the foreground, driven by Johnnie Lockett and Ken Miles, was the highest-placed car, coming in twelfth.

Left: Although this MGA engine appears relatively standard, it is one of the units which powered the EX 182s at Le Mans in 1955. It has a special Weslake cylinder head, 1.75 rather than 1.5 in twin carburettors, 9.4:1 compression ratio and no head gasket. It accordingly developed 82 rather than 68 bhp.

The MGA, as it appeared on announcement for the 1956 season. Thoroughly modern in concept, it replaced the ageing T-series line and, above all, was designed at Abingdon. It went on to become the world's best selling sports car.

who had drawn the original sketch on his kitchen table. Its 1.5 litre engine was effectively the same as that used in the Magnette.

The A looked good, handled well, had a top speed of 95 mph (152 km/h) and the public loved it. By the time that production ceased in 1962, over 100,000 examples of all variants had been completed, making it the most popular sports car in the world. Not only that; 91 per cent of As were exported, the overwhelming majority, as ever, going to America.

Cockpit of the MGA roadster. The distinctive layout of the steering wheel spokes echoed that of the EX 179 record-breaker. The horn button, unusually, was mounted in the centre of the dashboard.

In 1958 MG production reached a post-war record; it would climb even higher, and the 27,481 cars manufactured that year were well in excess of MG's entire pre-war output.

The MGA progressively evolved over its seven years of production. The 1600 version appeared in May 1959, engine capacity having been increased to 1,588cc and, again, to 1,622cc, in June 1961. The open car had been joined by a coupé version for 1957 and it was capable of 100 mph (160 km/h) on account of its aerodynamics being superior to the open cars.

In 1959 Phil Hill took the wheel of the last Abingdon-built record-breaker, the mid-engined EX 181 of 1957, which was powered by a supercharged 1.5 litre B-series-based twin overhead camshaft engine. On the Bonneville Salt Flats in Utah, USA, Hill achieved 254.91 mph (394 km/h), making it the fastest MG ever.

This engine, in unblown form, had been used in a faster version of the MGA, where it developed 108 bhp, as opposed to the 79 of its pushrod equivalent. The Twin Cam of 1958 was outwardly similar to the mainstream models although it was fitted with handsome Dunlop disc wheels and used all round disc brakes. This was a 110 mph (177 km/h) model but, unfortunately, it developed a reputation for unreliability and only 2,111 examples were produced in two years.

However, the MGA continued to perform well in international competition. There were class wins at Le Mans in 1960, at the 1961 Sebring Twelve Hours race in the United States and again in the 1962 Monte Carlo and Tulip Rallies.

The MGA Twin Cam is identifiable by its knock-off centrelock Dunlop wheels. Available in roadster and coupé form, this example was photographed at the MG Car Club's meeting at Brands Hatch in 1975 to commemorate the twentieth anniversary of the A's introduction.

MGA at Le Mans in 1960: a twin cam roadster having been converted to a coupé by MG for the race. For diplomatic reasons it was entered by the North Western Centre of the MG Car Club, being driven by Ted Lund and Colin Escott. The A ran faultlessly: they won the 2 litre class and were placed thirteenth overall.

MGB MASTERPIECE

I N 1957 work began on the A's replacement, coded EX 214, which was launched at the 1962 Motor Show. What could only be named the MGB was to be even more successful than its predecessor, over 500,000 being built, and it was to be the most popular MG in the history of the company.

But there was a bitter-sweet ingredient to this figure – the calamitous outcome of the financial problems experienced by MG's BMC parent. So the MGB remained in production for eighteen long years, by which time it had become progressively uncompetitive. Nonetheless, volumes did not peak until 1972, no fewer than ten years after its introduction. That year also represented an all-time annual production record for Abingdon, which saw the completion of 55,639 MGs.

John Thornley and Syd Enever were respectively responsible for the concept and engineering of the model. One of the reasons for the car's success was that, although derived from the MGA, an out-and-out sports car, the B was better equipped and intended to appeal to a broader spectrum of the public. It therefore had wind-up windows, rather than the rudimentary sliding side screens, and there was even a carpeted space for two small children behind the front seats.

Thornley's intention was to produce a car 'that no managing director would be ashamed to leave in his company car park' and his inspiration was the Aston Martin DB 2/4 coupé. Whilst the B could not have been anything but an open model on its launch, work was soon underway on a closed version.

Following MGA precedent, the stylistic concept of the MGB was Syd Enever's, with input from chief body engineer Jim O'Neill; the design was refined by Don Hayter, who in 1956 had joined MG from Aston Martin and prior to that Pressed Steel. It says much for the quality of their work that the model's lines had not dated appreciably when the end eventually came in 1980.

The B was powered by a 1.8 version of the B-series unit, a unique capacity and available only to MG until the arrival, in the 1965 season, of the Austin 1800 saloon. It made Abingdon's latest product a 103 mph (165 km/h) car, and more powerful than its predecessor.

Opposite:
A 1967 MGB, as owned by Roger Jerram.

Top: The MGB, as announced in September 1962, with its hood raised. The spot lamps were an optional extra, as were the wire wheels, discs being the norm.

Middle: The MGB GT arrived for 1966 and it remained in production until 1980. This example dates from 1975, with the appearance of energy-absorbing 'rubber' bumpers. It was photographed at the National Motor Museum, Beaulieu, with an Alfonso Hispano-Suiza in the foreground and a pre-war MG behind.

Bottom: The Midget as it appeared in 1961 was in essence a face-lifted Austin Healey Sprite. Note that the flat-topped rear wheel-arch does not match the front one, the result of MG and Healey being respectively responsible for the back and forward ends. Fortunately, when the cars were announced this inconsistency went unnoticed!

Its close derivative, named the MGB GT, arrived three years after the roadster for the 1966 season. Although it shared many body panels with the open car, Pininfarina, BMC's Italian styling consultant, put the finishing touches to the design, which emerged as a model in its own right.

Aimed at the family man, it was a car that his wife could also drive. There were small rear seats for the children and room for luggage, a shortcoming on the roadster, which was accessed by an opening rear

This works MGB ran at Le Mans in long-nose form in 1965. It was placed eleventh, the marque's highest post-war placing in the race, which was the last occasion a works B competed there. It is seen here at a revival meeting held at the Sarthe circuit.

The staff of MG's telephone exchange pose with a newly completed MGC, introduced for the 1968 season. Powered by BMC's 3 litre six-cylinder engine, it is identifiable by the bonnet bulge required to accommodate an enlarged radiator. Note the completed MGB roadster bodies arriving by transporter in the background.

31

If, as planned, the MGB had ceased production in 1970, this car, EX 234, built in 1964, would have replaced it. Styled by Pininfarina with Hydrolastic suspension and able to accommodate the B or A-series engines, it would also have taken the place of the MG Midget.

The MGB got its radiator grille back for the 1973 season, having been replaced by a corporate British Leyland recessed intake from the 1970 model year. This was when these Rostyle wheels replaced the original wires.

door, à la Aston Martin. The GT was to be a strong seller and would eventually account for 40 per cent of total B production.

By the nature of its engine capacity, the MGB could not be considered a replacement for the T-series cars. But in June 1961 matters were redressed with the arrival of the 948cc Midget. This is a car that began life in 1958 as the Austin Healey Sprite, a model conceived at Healey's Warwick design facility in the spirit of the Seven-based Austin Nippy of pre-war days. It was powered by a 948cc version of BMC's A-series engine, and a distinctive

As some 80 per cent of MGBs were exported to the United States, from 1967 Abingdon had to crash-test the model to evaluate whether it conformed to that country's increasingly stringent safety regulations.

feature was the cheeky 'Frogeye' front with protruding headlamps, which incorporated the wings, which hinged forward in one piece. Geoff Healey had been inspired by Jaguar's Le Mans-winning D-type in this regard. There was an economy-conscious rear end with no external access to the boot. Quarter-elliptic rear springs were adopted for the same reason.

Built at Abingdon from the outset, the Frogeye was followed in June 1961 by a Mark II model with a more conventional bonnet and opening boot. However, an MG version, which saw a revival of the Midget name, appeared later in the same month and at £669 cost £28 more. As a result the word 'Spridget' entered

Like the MGB, the Midget was also fitted with 'rubber' energy-absorbing bumpers for the 1975 season. Ride height was similarly raised.

33

the motoring language, having been first applied at Abingdon to pre-production hybrid Sprites fitted with MG Midget radiator grilles.

Capable of 85 mph (137 km/h), the Midget received a 1,098cc engine for the 1963 season. The more powerful Mark II version of March 1964 witnessed the appearance of half-elliptic rear springs, and the Mark III for 1,275cc Mini Cooper S engine. By this time the Midget's top speed exceeded 90 mph (145 km/h).

Although the Sprite had been similarly updated, it was effectively discontinued in 1969. But, as will emerge, this Healey-based MG was destined to outlive its progenitor.

BMC had, since 1958, concentrated all of its sports-car production at Abingdon. This meant that the Austin Healey 100/6, and its 3000 successor, were also built there until the model was discontinued in 1968.

Works MGBs continued to shine competitively. An example won the 2 litre class at Le Mans in 1963 and the same car then proceeded to triumph in the GT class of the 1964 Monte Carlo Rally. MGBs were the first British cars home at Sebring in the years between 1964 and 1968, the 1965 race excepted. Le Mans in 1964 and 1965 saw the cars from Abingdon come second in class, being outperformed only by Porsches. And a B won the new 1,000 Miles race at Brands Hatch in 1965.

A 1977 'rubber'-bumpered MGB roadster, with Midget in the background. A modest refinement was the fitting of quartz halogen headlamps.

Opposite:
The MGB GT V8 appeared late in 1972 and is identifiable by its wheels and the V8 badges on the front wings and the grille.

Outwardly the fortunes of MG's BMC parent appeared to be riding high, and in 1964 a Mini Cooper S won the Monte Carlo Rally for the first time. This success was to be repeated in 1966 and 1967. The cars were prepared by the BMC Competitions Department established in 1954 by Thornley at MG's Abingdon works. It was staffed by many of the personnel who could draw on their experiences of the great days of 1930–5 when MG's racing programme was in the ascendant.

The ubiquitous B-series engine had been extended in 1959 to the Mark III version of the Magnette saloon. This 1,489cc car was BMC's corporate four-door saloon styled by Pininfarina, and was variously offered with all of the Corporation's marque names. The Mark IV version arrived for 1962, having been enlarged to 1,622cc, but the line proved to be a poor seller, only 30,000 being built.

New striped seats, a revised facia and a new, smaller steering wheel were notable features of the 1977 model year MGB. These features endured until the end of production in 1980.

MG ascendant? An MGB takes to the air at the MG sports ground in Abingdon on the occasion of the fiftieth anniversary celebrations of the company's arrival in the town, held over the weekend of 8th/9th September 1979. Official news of the factory's closure broke on Monday the 10th.

By contrast, the MG 1100, a badge-engineered version of the Issigonis-designed, Pininfarina-styled, front-wheel-drive Morris 1100 of 1962, was to prove a hit with the public although it was built at Cowley. Uprated with twin carburettors and an enhanced interior, it was both faster and more accelerative than the Morris version, being capable of 85 mph (136 km/h). A grand total of 157,409 examples had been sold by the time production ceased in 1973. Originally available in 1,098cc form, it was enlarged to 1,275cc in 1967 and became the MG 1300.

At the 1967 Motor Show BMC unveiled a derivative of the MGB in the form of the MGC. Powered by a 3 litre engine intended for an Austin Healey replacement that was never produced, the C transformed the B into a 120 mph (193 km/h) car. But the heavy power unit affected handling and a mere 9,000 roadsters and GTs were completed before production ceased in 1969.

By this time BMC's financial problems had boiled over. It had, among many other woes, drastically under-priced the sophisticated, popular Mini and its top-selling 1100 derivative. As a consequence, in 1968, it was taken over by the Leyland Corporation, which already owned the rival Triumph marque and also Rover.

Inevitably British Leyland's new management favoured Triumph, and MG was left to make do with its sound but increasingly uncompetitive MGB, an echo of the hiatus of the 1952–5 era. John Thornley left Abingdon at this time, retiring in 1969 from ill health. Corporate sports-car funding was switched to Triumph and the outcome was the stylistically and mechanically flawed TR7 coupé of 1975.

As will have been apparent, MG was very dependent upon the American market for much of its production and from 1968 transatlantic emissions and safety regulations began to impinge on the models' specification. This became outwardly apparent from the 1975 model year when the B and Midget were fitted with energy-absorbing 'rubber' (in reality polyurethane) bumpers.

Not only did this add weight to the car but American regulations required that the headlamps should be 16 to 20 inches (406 to 508 mm) above the ground. As the MGB did not conform, it was necessary to increase the ride height by 1.5 inches (38.1mm), achieved by packing the front suspension and increasing the camber of the rear springs. This was to induce undesirable body roll, a problem which was addressed from 1976 by the fitment of a rear anti-roll bar and uprating the front one.

Yet another MGB derivative appeared in August 1973 although it was available only as a GT. The MGB GT V8 was powered by the now in-house Rover 3.5 litre V8 engine. Although capable of 125 mph (201 km/h), this ageing model was expensive at £2,294 and the international oil crisis, which erupted in October of that year, provided the knock-out blow. Only 2,591 examples were completed before production ceased in the autumn of 1976.

Spiralling oil prices and the resultant recession triggered the collapse of British Leyland late in 1974. It was nationalised in the following year and

The Abingdon compound in 1980. The MGB GTs in the foreground are examples of the LE (Limited Edition) version offered to British customers for the 1981 season. The roadster version is in the background. Also note Triumph TR7s and a lone Rover SD1.

Opposite:
A batch of MGB independent front-suspension units, complete with disc brakes and anti-roll bars, awaiting fitment at Abingdon in 1980.

End of the line on
22nd October
1980. The notice
on this MGB's
windscreen reads
'The Last One?'
It wasn't; but this
Japan-bound car
in porcelain white
with black interior
was the final
roadster to be
exported.

The two
individuals most
closely associated
with the MGB
stand by the last
car to leave the
Abingdon
production line
on 23rd October
1980. Former
general manager
John Thornley
(left) with his
own GT, complete
with its famous
registration
number, and one-
time chief engineer
Syd Enever with
the ultimate
Pewter Metallic
MGB GT. It was
destined for the
Heritage Motor
Centre at Gaydon,
Warwickshire.

Gate 3 of MG's Abingdon factory on the Marcham Road in 1980, the year of the plant's closure.

renamed Leyland Cars. The business drifted until 1977, when Michael Edwardes took over as chairman. The firm became BL Cars, allowing the marque names to flourish once again.

However, Edwardes embarked on a series of factory closures and one of these was the MG plant at Abingdon. The news, announced on 10th September 1979, caused a universal outcry but went ahead nonetheless. The last Midget, from 1975 powered by the 1.5 litre Triumph engine shared with the Spitfire, was built in December 1979.

The MGB survived for a further ten months and the last car, a Pewter Metallic GT, was completed on Wednesday 22nd October 1980. A sombre ceremony, attended by John Thornley and Syd Enever, took place on the following day when the final car was seen off the line. The workforce signed off for the last time on the Friday and, after fifty-one years, the Abingdon-built MG was no more.

The same location in 1981. On the right is A Block, where the cars were assembled, which survived for some time. Today the town's new police station occupies the site.

REBIRTH OF THE MGB

THERE was a nineteen-month hiatus between the end of the MGB and the arrival, in May 1982, of the next MG model. From that time on practically all MGs would be built at the former Austin factory at Longbridge, near Birmingham.

The new model was a faster version of the Austin Metro hatchback, the so-called Supermini which had been well received on its introduction in 1980. The MG was a 100 mph (160 km/h) car, thanks to a tuned 72 bhp engine, and there were smart alloy wheels. It survived until 1990, by which time over 120,000 had found customers.

A potent but fragile 93 bhp turbocharged version appeared for 1983 but only 21,968 were built before production ceased in 1989.

The mechanically unrelated mid-engined Metro 6R4 Group B rally car of 1984 also bore the MG badge. A four-wheel-drive car using a bespoke 3 litre 38 bhp V6 with twin-cam cylinder heads, it failed to win a major event. Some two hundred had been completed by 1987.

In March 1983 BL launched the 1.6 litre Austin Maestro hatchback but the faster MG version with twin Weber carburettors was an unpredictable runner. Only 2,762 were made, although an improved 2 litre version of 1984–91 fared a little better.

The 2 litre Austin Montego, the saloon version of the Maestro, appeared in April 1984 and was a popular car although the MG variant was again relatively scarce and only 38,000 or so were built. Like the hatchback, there was a turbocharged model of 1985 but a 124 mph (199 km/h) top speed did not mitigate the mediocre handling, the result of 150 bhp of power passing through the front wheels. It lasted until 1991. And it was a similar story with the Maestro Turbo of 1989, which was even scarcer: just 505 were sold.

By then the parent company's status had changed yet again. In 1986 the BL name had been replaced by that of The Rover Group, indicative of a move up market. Then in 1988 the company, after thirteen years of British government ownership, was purchased by aircraft manufacturer British Aerospace.

Opposite:
A pre-production MG RV8 photographed in Wales, prior to the model's launch at the 1992 Birmingham Motor Show. The RV8 was produced in right-hand-drive form only, and the quality of the trim and wood-grained dashboard speaks for itself.

Above:
Introduced in May 1982, the popular MG version of the successful Metro Supermini was instantly identifiable by its striking livery, alloy wheels and red seat-belts. Less apparent was the tweaked suspension. The 72 bhp engine delivered 100 mph (160 km/h) performance.

The MG Maestro, a variation on the Austin theme, started life in 1.6 litre form in 1983 but was re-launched in 1984 in 2 litre EFi guise and survived until 1991. This is the 1987 version.

As will have been clear, the MG name had been maintained by badge-engineered versions of existing models. However, interest in the marque was heightened with the surprise appearance, at the 1985 Frankfurt Motor Show, of the MG EX-E concept car.

The MG Montego Turbo of 1985 was a low-volume version of the 1984 MG Montego. With a top speed of 128 mph (206 km/h), it was the fastest of this generation of MG saloons.

MG RV8 bodies taking shape at British Motor Heritage's facility at Faringdon, Oxfordshire in 1993. They were then transported to Cowley for final assembly.

This visually stunning example of blue-sky thinking saw a new V6 engine theoretically united with the Metro 6R4's four-wheel drive. Although EX-E's acclaimed lines were credited to Rover's chief corporate stylist, Roy Axe, it was actually the work of his young colleague Gerry McGovern.

The MG badge was redesigned for the RV8 and it reverted to the chocolate and cream livery used from the 1928 season until 1962, when the MGB was given a red background.

There was no question of putting EX-E into production but in 1992 the MG name, for the first time in twelve years, was once again solely applied to a sports car. That year's Motor Show saw the launch of the MG RV8, its arrival being timed to commemorate the thirtieth anniversary of the MGB's appearance at the 1962 event.

This was wholly appropriate because the 'new' model was also MGB-based. Its starting point was a replacement roadster body shell pressed from the original tooling that Rover's subsidiary, British Motor Heritage, had been producing since 1988 for enthusiasts. Power came from the proven and seemingly evergreen Rover V8, by then enlarged to 3.9 litres.

The MG RV8 was planned as a low volume model; only some 1,983 examples were completed between 1993 and 1995 at a special facility established at Rover's Cowley factory. Unlike the original MGB, this was an expensive car, selling for £25,440.

It was able to attain 135 mph (217 km/h), and build quality was not in question but British customers did not respond in the expected numbers and

The MG RV8 was intended to represent how the MGB might have evolved had not production ceased in 1980. The family resemblance between the two cars is well illustrated.

80 per cent of cars, 1,568 no less, were shipped to the Far East, the model being favoured by Japanese enthusiasts. However, the MG RV8 had another role and that was to prepare the way for the wholly new MG*F* sports car, which was launched, to universal acclaim, at the 1995 Geneva Motor Show.

By then Rover had yet another new owner, BMW having purchased the company from British Aerospace in 1994 for £800 million. How would MG fare under German ownership?

Opposite:
A display version of the RV8's 3.9 litre Rover V8 engine.

THE ROAD TO NANJING

THE MGF was the first wholly new MG sports car since the introduction of the MGB of 1962, and its short-nose/high-tail styling reflected a mid-located engine. Rover's new chief stylist, Gerry McGovern, had produced a distinctive shape that looked like no other car. It also had the virtue of being the world's first affordable mid-engined roadster and, above all, it was all British, unlike its saloon stable-mates, which had been developed in conjunction with Honda, BL's one-time engineering partner.

The days of high-volume models, however, had gone. Rover planned to build 12,000 MGFs a year. The engineering team was led by Brian Griffin and, later, Nick Fell. The engine was the company's own 1.8 litre aluminium K-series unit with twin overhead camshafts, it being mounted transversely behind the driving compartment. This location, and all independent Moulton Hydrogas suspension, endowed the new MG with excellent road holding.

It was available in two forms: the basic model, which cost £15,995, could attain 120 mph (193 km/h), but a more powerful VVC (variable valve control) version cost £2,000 more and was capable of 130 mph (209 km/h).

The introduction of the MGF marked the rebirth of the marque and in 1995 Rover established MG Cars, a subsidiary to handle its sales. In 1996, the first full year of production, the model emerged as Britain's bestselling sports car, appealing to both men and women, a pole position it would retain for much of its production life. Although exported, it did not sell in MG's traditional American market because Rover had lacked the financial resources to allow it to be specially engineered. However, further refinement followed for 2000 with the arrival of Steptronic automatic transmission.

But after six years ownership, and against the background of mounting losses, in March 2000 news broke that BMW wanted to divest itself of Rover. It was acquired in May for a token £10 by the British-owned Phoenix Consortium, which possessed just one car factory: the former Austin plant at Longbridge.

Opposite:
A line-up of MGFs at the model's second birthday party in September 1997. It was staged by MG Cars at the Heritage Motor Centre, Gaydon.

Gerry McGovern, who was responsible for the MGF's distinctive lines, with the E-EX concept of 1985, which he also styled and which represented the visual starting-point for the new model.

An MGF body under construction at the Motor Panels factory in Coventry in 1995. Its Mayflower Corporation parent invested some £24.2 million for the project. The unpainted shells were then delivered, eight at a time, to the West Works at Longbridge.

In September the business was renamed MG Rover and in April 2001 MG Sport & Racing was formed with the sub-brand of MG X Power intended to symbolise its competition activities.

The most ambitious of these was a return to Le Mans in 2001 but the Lola-based EX 257 did not finish and the two entrants in 2002 were also unsuccessful.

BMW's ownership of Rover had also meant that the MG badge could be applied only to sports cars, so as not to clash with its respected sports saloons. So the policy, also initiated in 1992, was set aside and the MG name moved to the fore on more potent versions of the Rover line.

In 2001 the front-wheel-drive 25 hatchback (introduced in 1996), 45 hatchback/saloon (1995), 75 saloon (1998) and the newly launched estate version were respectively designated ZR, ZS, ZT and ZT-T. They were instantly identifiable by painted, rather than chromed, radiator shells. A further expansion of the MGF family came in 2001 with the option of an entry-level 1.6 litre engine. Later, for 2003, the saloons were also available in turbocharged 2 litre diesel form.

The MGF was approaching its seventh birthday in January 2002 when the company unveiled the MGTF with a new, inclined nose and multi-link rear suspension.

The MG XPower SV appeared at that year's Motor Show, based on the Qvale Mangusta, MG Rover having purchased the Italian manufacturer in 2001. It was powered by a Ford Mustang-based 4.6 litre V8 engine and had a top speed of 195 mph (313 km/h) but a price tag of £65,000 ensured that there were few takers even though this was the fastest MG road car in history.

In 2001 MG Rover launched ZS EX 259, based on the MGZS 2.0KV6, with two cars driven by Anthony Reid (left) and Warren Hughes. Tailored for the British Touring Car Championship, sadly they failed to make much impact.

An MG Lola EX 257 at Le Mans in 2002. Two cars were entered but both dropped out with transmission problems. This one driven by Blundell, Bailey and McGarrity, survived until the early hours of Sunday morning, the event having started at 4pm on the Saturday.

However, modest production levels and an ageing car range made the company's prospects look increasingly bleak. In June 2004 partnership talks began with the state-owned Shanghai Automotive Industry Corporation (SAIC) of China but these ultimately collapsed. As a consequence the end for MG Rover came on 7th April 2005, and with it went Britain's indigenous motor industry as a volume producer of cars.

This might have appeared to have been the end of MG, but in July 2005 the name and manufacturing rights were purchased for £53 million by Shanghai's rival, the Nanjing Automobile Corporation, which was also a nationalised business. It then proceeded to dismantle the Longbridge production lines and rebuild them in China.

The MG range of 2001 pictured at MG Rover's international headquarters, Longbridge. Left to right: MG ZT-T, MG ZT, MG ZS, MG ZR and MGF.

The MGF was given a facelift in 2002 with the arrival of the MGTF with a new nose, echoing the TF of 1954/5 vintage, and revised suspension to the benefit of roadholding. This is the Cool Blue SE version with optional tonneau cover. *Coronation Street* TV star Tracy Shaw is at the wheel.

Rover's all-alloy 24-valve KV6 engine dated from 1996 and was available as an optional fitment, in 2 and 2.5 litre forms respectively, in the MG ZS and ZT saloons (*left*). This photograph was taken at Longbridge in October 2001 to commemorate the production by Powertrain Ltd of the 100,000th example.

Intended as an MG flagship, the potent 4.8 litre Ford V8-powered XPower SV, capable of around 170 mph (273 km/h), was unveiled at the 2002 Motor Show. But with prices starting at £65,000 there were few takers.

The first Nanjing-built MG*TF*, having been completed in March 2007, was priced between 180,000 and 400,000 yuan (£11,800 to £26,400). This equates to about two years' salary for Chinese workers.

The company then shipped kits of parts to Britain and the first example was symbolically completed at Longbridge on 29th May 2007. Then the onetime rival Nanjing and Shanghai businesses merged in 2008, delaying the arrival of the Longbridge-assembled MG*TF*, still imminent at the time of publication.

A second Nanjing-built car, titled the MG7L, previously the Rover 75-based ZT saloon, went on sale in China in the autumn of 2007. With further models promised, Nanjing is predicting global sales of 200,000 cars per annum by 2012. If this sounds unduly optimistic, who would ever have predicted MG ending up in Chinese ownership?

The Chinese-built MG*TF* unveiled by Nanjing Automobile on 27th March 2007. The Chinese characters 'MG' are pronounced Ming Gue, which means 'a famous high-ranked person', a far cry from Morris Garages!

FURTHER INFORMATION

FURTHER READING

Allison, Mike. *MG: The Magic of the Marque*. Dalton Watson, 1989.
Barraclough, R. I., and Jennings, P. L. *Oxford to Abingdon*. Myrtle Publishing, 1998.
Haining, Peter, (editor). *The MG Log*. Souvenir Press, 1993.
Jennings, P. L. *Early MG*. Privately published, 1989.
Knowles, David. *MG: The Untold Story*. Windrow & Green, 1997.
McComb, F. Wilson. *MG by McComb*. Osprey, 1978, 1984 and 1998.
The New England MGT Register. *The Kimber Centenary Book*, 1988.
Thornley, John. *Maintaining the Breed*. Motor Racing Publications, 1950, 1956 and 1991.
Wood, Jonathan. *MG from A to Z*. Motor Racing Publications, 1998.

Journal:
MG Enthusiast, Hothouse Publishing, First Floor, 2 King Street, Peterborough PE1 1LT. Telephone: 01733 246500. Website: www.mgenthusiast.com.

CLUBS

MG Car Club, Kimber House, PO Box 251, Abingdon, Oxfordshire OX14 1FF. Telephone: 01235 555552. Website: www.mgcc.co.uk
MG Octagon Car Club, Harry Crutchley, Units 1-3, Parchfields Enterprise Park, Parchfields Farm, Colton Road, Trent Valley, Rugeley, Staffordshire WS15 3HB. Telephone: 01889 574666. Website: www.mgoctagoncarclub.com For pre-1956 cars.
MG Owners' Club, Octagon House, I Over Road, Swavesey, Cambridge CB24 4QZ. Telephone: 01954 231125. Website: www.mgcars.org.uk/mgoc

PLACES TO VISIT

Museum displays may be altered and readers are advised to check before travelling that the relevant vehicles are on show and to ascertain the opening times. An up-to-date listing of all road-transport museums in the United Kingdom can be found on www.motormuseums.com
Haynes International Motor Museum, Sparkford, Yeovil, Somerset BA22 7LH. Telephone: 01963 440804. Website: www.haynesmotormuseum.co.uk
Heritage Motor Centre, Banbury Road, Gaydon, Warwickshire CV35 0BJ. Telephone: 01926 641888. Website: www.heritage-motor-centre.co.uk
National Motor Museum, John Montagu Building, Beaulieu, Brockenhurst, Hampshire SO42 7ZN. Telephone: 01590 612345. Website: www.beaulieu.co.uk

A MG Super Sports 14/28 of June 1924 with body by Carbodies, although it would have borne a Morris Garages body plate. Note Kimber's distinctive triangulated windscreen supports and scuttle-mounted ship's ventilator-style air intakes.

INDEX

Page numbers in italic refer to illustrations